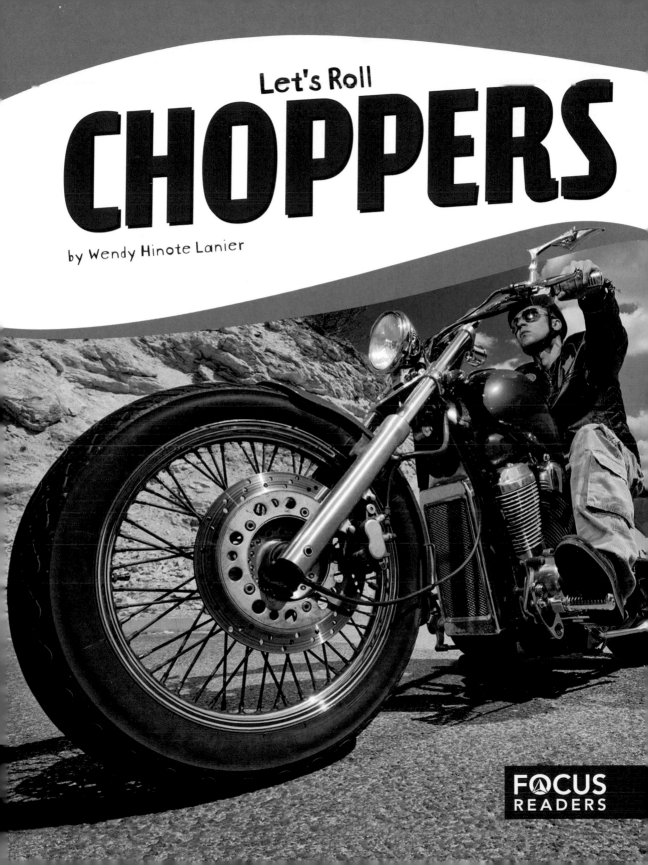

Let's Roll

CHOPPERS

by Wendy Hinote Lanier

FOCUS READERS

www.northstareditions.com

Produced for North Star Editions by Red Line Editorial.

Photographs ©: Ljupco Smokovski/Shutterstock Images, cover, 1; Joseph Sohm/Shutterstock Images, 4–5, 7; NanoStock/Shutterstock Images, 8; Library of Congress, 10–11; Tracey Stearns/Shutterstock Images, 13, 29; Uncleroo/Shutterstock Images, 14; Wollertz/Shutterstock Images, 16–17; James Steidl/Shutterstock Images, 18; Click and Photo/Shutterstock Images, 20; Andrey Armyagov/Shutterstock Images, 22–23; holbox/Shutterstock Images, 25; Fernando Blanco Calzada/Shutterstock Images, 26–27

ISBN
978-1-63517-054-2 (hardcover)
978-1-63517-110-5 (paperback)
978-1-63517-211-9 (ebook pdf)
978-1-63517-161-7 (hosted ebook)

Library of Congress Control Number: 2016951016

Printed in the United States of America
Mankato, MN
November, 2016

About the Author

Wendy Hinote Lanier is a native Texan and former elementary teacher who writes and speaks to children and adults on a variety of topics. She is the author of more than 20 books for children and young people. Some of her favorite people are dogs.

TABLE OF CONTENTS

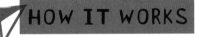

CHAPTER 1

ROLLING INTO STURGIS

A sunny August morning dawns in Sturgis, South Dakota. Hundreds of thousands of motorcycles roll into the tiny town. Most of them are choppers. The annual Sturgis Motorcycle Rally is in full swing.

> **The streets of Sturgis are packed with choppers at the annual motorcycle rally.**

5

Lines of motorcycles head out on bike tours. The tours wind their way along scenic roads in the Black Hills. In downtown Sturgis, the historic Main Street is open only to motorcycles. Choppers are parked side by side down the middle and on both sides of the street.

FUN FACT

Attendance at the Sturgis Motorcycle Rally has reached more than 600,000. The town's usual population is approximately 6,700.

 Riders take in the scenery of South Dakota's famous Black Hills.

> **Riders come from all around the world to attend the Sturgis Motorcycle Rally.**

In the afternoons, crowds gather at the Sturgis Dragway to watch races. People have to shout to be heard over all the noise. Other bikers test their skills in hill-climbing competitions. As the sun sets on Sturgis, there are outdoor concerts. For more than a week, the town of Sturgis is a chopper lover's paradise.

THE FIRST STURGIS RALLY

The original Sturgis Motorcycle Rally took place in 1938. It was started by J. C. "Pappy" Hoel, the owner of a local motorcycle shop. The original rally featured a race. There were also dangerous stunts such as ramp jumps and head-on collisions with cars.

CHAPTER 2

CHOPPER HISTORY

Almost as soon as motorcycles were invented, people began racing them. To improve speed and performance, riders stripped their bikes of everything that wasn't necessary.

 A crowd gathers to watch a motorcycle race in the 1920s.

Parts that could not be removed were shortened, or bobbed. Motorcycles stripped down for racing were called bobbers.

After World War II (1939–1945), many US soldiers returned home with mechanical skills they had learned in the military. They used these skills to add special features

▷ **Custom choppers can have extreme raking.**

to their motorcycles. They replaced exhaust systems with straight pipes. They began **raking** the front end so the front tire was farther from the bike. They also chopped and lowered the bike's frame.

Chopper owners sometimes ride in large groups.

By the 1970s, these chopped-up
and reworked bikes were known
as choppers.

Choppers attracted biker gangs
that did not always follow the

rules. Choppers and their owners became known as the outlaws of the motorcycle world.

HARLEY-DAVIDSON

Choppers can be made from any type of motorcycle, but the most popular is Harley-Davidson. Early Harley-Davidson models were built primarily for racing. But during the 1950s, Harley-Davidsons became a favorite to ride and **customize**. The Harley 74 was especially popular because it was easy to repair. It was also easy to modify, which meant it could reflect the owner's personality.

CHAPTER 3

WHAT MAKES A CHOPPER?

No two choppers are alike. But certain features are common on just about all of them. Choppers are custom-made motorcycles. Very few choppers are built for racing or trail riding.

Chopper owners often add personalized touches to their bikes to make them unique.

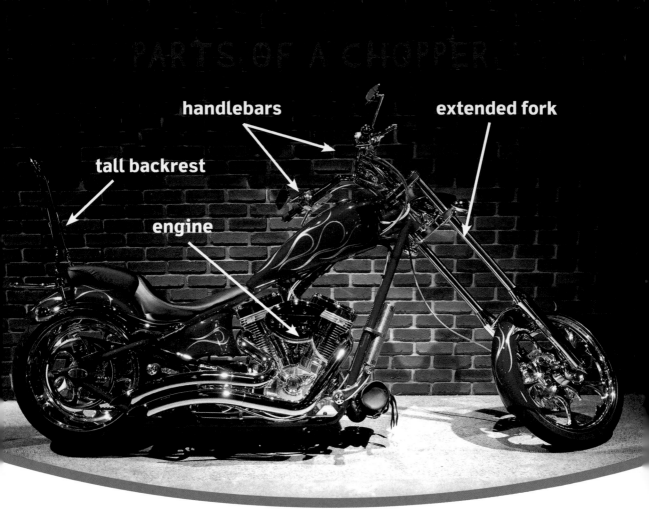

PARTS OF A CHOPPER

handlebars

extended fork

tall backrest

engine

Instead, they are designed to cruise

the roads in style.

Most choppers feature extended

forks, no front fender, narrow

seats, and wide rear tires. There is usually no rear **suspension**, and the bike rides low to the ground. Many choppers have long, high handlebars called ape hangers. Tall backrests are also common.

APE HANGERS

Many states have laws that regulate ape hanger handlebars. Handlebars can usually be no higher than the rider's shoulder height. However, many bikers believe that high handlebars improve performance and are more comfortable.

 A biker cruises the streets with his ape hangers.

Sometimes choppers are made from scratch. Often they are made by chopping up a **stock bike** and adding personalized details. But they are almost always colorful, and they tend to match the personalities of their owners.

FUN FACT

The name "ape hangers" comes from the way riders hold the handlebars. It is similar to the way an ape hangs from a tree.

CHAPTER 4

TODAY'S CHOPPER

The chopper world has changed a lot since the 1960s. Chopper owners used to be the bad boys of motorcycling. Today's owners are just as likely to be doctors and lawyers who ride on the weekends.

 The number of women who ride choppers continues to grow.

These days, many choppers are factory custom bikes. These are stock bikes that have the basic chopper shape. Owners can change out parts and **accessories** for a custom look.

But many chopper owners still prefer to chop up a factory bike.

FUN FACT

A custom chopper made by a specialty company can cost more than $20,000.

 Many choppers have elaborate paint jobs featuring flames.

Others hire small companies to design and build a bike from the ground up. The frame and all the parts are fabricated on site. The result is a rolling work of art.

COMPUTER-AIDED DESIGN

Companies that build custom choppers use computer-aided design and manufacturing software to create one-of-a-kind bikes. Computer-designed parts are cut using waterjet cutting tools. Other parts are cut using a process called multiaxis machining. This involves pieces of machinery that rotate cutting tools or parts to shape them. Computers control the machines' movements to create perfect parts every time.

Computer-aided design helps companies make high-quality parts.

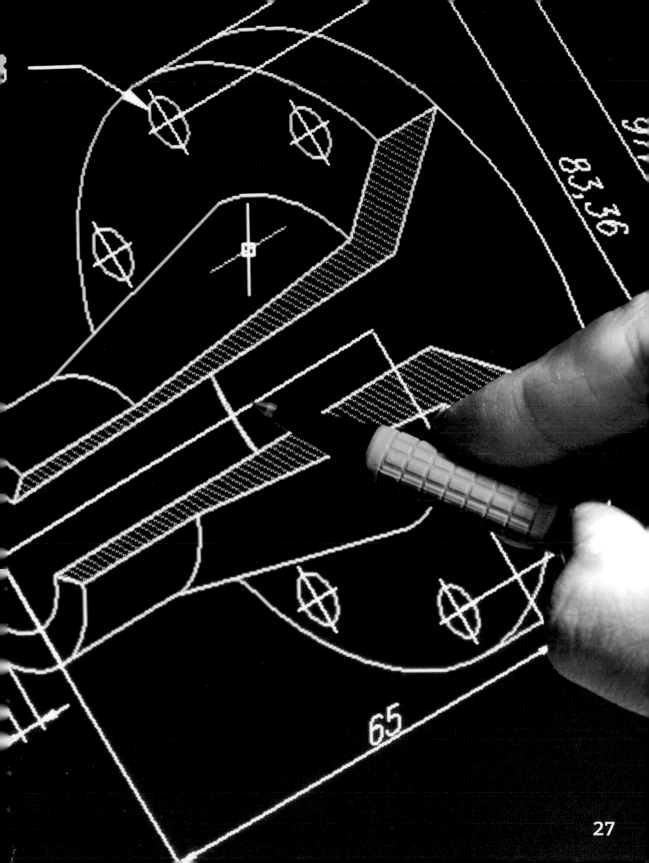

FOCUS ON
CHOPPERS

Write your answers on a separate piece of paper.

1. Write a sentence that summarizes the main idea of Chapter 2.

2. Would you want to attend the Sturgis Motorcycle Rally? Why or why not?

3. What do chopper owners call long, high handlebars?

    A. ape hangers

    B. forks

    C. suspension

4. Why would a chopper owner most likely add accessories to her bike?

    A. to make the bike quieter

    B. to make the bike look unique

    C. to make the bike go faster

5. What does **outlaws** mean in this book?

    A. people who own several motorcycles

    B. people who do not follow rules

    C. people who travel in large groups

Choppers attracted biker gangs that did not always follow the rules. Choppers and their owners became known as the **outlaws** of the motorcycle world.

6. What does **fabricated** mean in this book?

    A. hired a company

    B. removed the frame

    C. made using skill

Others hire small companies to design and build a bike from the ground up. The frame and all the parts are **fabricated** on site.

Answer key on page 32.

GLOSSARY

accessories
Extra parts that are added for convenience, attractiveness, or safety.

customize
To build something according to a person's plan or design.

forks
The metal tubes that attach the front wheel of a motorcycle to the frame.

raking
Increasing the angle or distance of the front wheel from the frame.

stock bike
A motorcycle that is made by the manufacturer with no input from the buyer.

suspension
A system for cushioning bumps and making a vehicle's ride smoother.

TO LEARN MORE

BOOKS

Hamilton, John. *Choppers*. Minneapolis: Abdo Publishing Company, 2014.

Monnig, Alex. *Behind the Wheel of a Chopper*. Mankato, MN: The Child's World, 2016.

Savage, Jeff. *Choppers*. Mankato, MN: Capstone Press, 2010.

NOTE TO EDUCATORS

Visit **www.focusreaders.com** to find lesson plans, activities, links, and other resources related to this title.

INDEX

Answer Key: 1. Answers will vary; 2. Answers will vary; 3. A; 4. B; 5. B; 6. C